Psychology and Manipulation in Politics and Media

CRITICAL THINKING ABSENCE FROM MARX AND GRAMSCI TO AI ERA

IGOR BARTAK

Igor Bartak

Psychology and Manipulation in Politics and Media

REAL FANTASY

CONTENTS:

FOREWORD

The intersection of psychology, politics, and media manipulation is a complex field that explores how psychological principles are employed to influence public opinion, behavior, and decision-making. This manipulation can take various forms, from emotional appeals to the strategic use of misinformation.

Dark psychology, which encompasses traits like narcissism, Machiavellianism, and psychopathy, plays a significant role in political manipulation. Politicians often exploit these traits to gain power and control over their constituents. For example:

- **Narcissism**: Politicians with narcissistic tendencies may create an "us vs. them" narrative, fostering loyalty among their supporters while alienating opponents.

- **Machiavellianism**: This involves cunning strategies such as political triangulation, where leaders position themselves as neutral to appeal to a wider audience while undermining adversaries.

- **Psychopathy**: Fearmongering is a common tactic used by psychopathic leaders who exaggerate threats (e.g., immigration or terrorism) to consolidate power by positioning themselves as the sole solution.

Politicians frequently utilize **emotional appeals** to connect with voters. By eliciting emotions such as fear, anger, or hope, they can sway public opinion effectively. Techniques include:

- **Fear Appeals**: Highlighting threats can lead the public to seek strong leadership for protection.
- **Primacy and Recency Effects**: These cognitive biases suggest that people remember the first and last pieces of information best, allowing politicians to craft messages for maximum impact.

Media serves as a powerful tool for political manipulation. Various strategies are employed to shape narratives and influence public perception:

- **Illusory Truth Effect**: Repeated exposure to false claims can lead individuals to accept them as true over time.
- **Scandal Distraction**: Politicians may create minor scandals to divert attention from more significant issues, manipulating the news cycle.

- **Astroturfing**: This involves creating the illusion of grassroots support for a cause or candidate through coordinated efforts on social media platforms.

The interplay between psychology and manipulation in politics and media highlights the profound impact of emotional appeals and cognitive biases on public perception. Understanding these mechanisms is crucial for recognizing how political narratives are crafted and disseminated in contemporary society. As citizens become more aware of these tactics, they can better navigate the complexities of political communication and media influence.

Igor Bartak

ANTONIO GRAMSCI AND CULTURAL HEGEMONY

Antonio Gramsci was a key influential Italian Marxist philosopher, linguist, journalist, and politician, born on January 22, 1891, in Ales, Sardinia. He is best known for his theory of **cultural hegemony**, which describes how the ruling classes maintain power not through force but by shaping cultural norms and ideologies that become accepted as common sense within society. Gramsci's political career included being a founding member of the Italian Communist Party, and he was a vocal critic of Benito Mussolini's fascist regime. After his arrest in 1926, he spent much of his life in prison, where he wrote extensively, producing over 3,000 pages of analysis and theory before his death in 1937.

Gramsci's Views on Media

Gramsci's insights into media are particularly relevant today as they highlight the role of cultural institutions in maintaining power dynamics. He argued that the ruling class uses media to propagate its ideology and values, effectively controlling public perception and discourse. This manipulation leads to what he termed "consent," where the working class unknowingly supports the status quo because they accept the dominant ideology as natural or beneficial.

Key Concepts

- **Cultural Hegemony**: Gramsci posited that the ruling class maintains control by establishing a dominant culture that shapes societal norms and values. This cultural dominance is achieved through institutions like media, education, and religion.

- **Role of Media**: In Gramsci's framework, media acts as a powerful tool for disseminating hegemonic ideas. It serves to reinforce the existing social order by promoting narratives that align with the interests of the elites. For instance, contemporary social media platforms can amplify specific messages that support capitalist ideologies and consumerism.

- **Manufacturing Consent**: Gramsci believed that consent is manufactured through cultural means rather than coercive force. This process involves creating a "common sense" understanding among the populace that aligns with elite interests. The media plays a crucial role in this by framing issues in ways that favor the status quo.

Contemporary Relevance

Gramsci's theories remain pertinent as they provide a lens through which to analyze modern media dynamics. With the rise of social media, elites can now influence public opinion on a global scale more effectively than ever before. The control over information dissemination by tech giants mirrors Gramsci's concerns about how cultural institutions can shape societal beliefs and behaviors.

In summary, Antonio Gramsci's work emphasizes the importance of cultural hegemony and the role of media in reinforcing power structures, making his insights invaluable for understanding contemporary society's dynamics.

Long March through the Institutions

Antonio Gramsci's concept of the "Long March through the Institutions" is rooted in his broader theory of **cultural hegemony**, which he developed during his imprisonment under Mussolini's regime. Although the phrase itself was popularized later by Rudi Dutschke in the 1960s, it reflects Gramsci's ideas about how societal change can be achieved through gradual infiltration and transformation of cultural institutions rather than through violent revolution.

Cultural Hegemony

Gramsci argued that the ruling class, or bourgeoisie, maintains its power not merely through economic means or coercion but by establishing a dominant culture that shapes societal norms and values. This cultural dominance is achieved through various institutions, including education, media, religion, and the arts.

By controlling these institutions, the ruling class can propagate its ideology and ensure that it becomes accepted as common sense among the populace.

Impact on Institutions

The "Long March through the Institutions" refers to a strategic approach aimed at gradually gaining influence within key societal structures. Gramsci believed that for a revolutionary movement to succeed, it must first gain control over cultural institutions to reshape public consciousness. This involves working within existing frameworks—such as schools, universities, churches, and media—to promote alternative ideologies and values that challenge the dominant culture.

Gradual Transformation

Rather than advocating for an immediate overthrow of the existing order, Gramsci emphasized a slow and systematic process of change. This approach allows for the development of a counter-hegemony—an alternative set of beliefs and practices that can eventually replace those of the ruling class. By cultivating new intellectuals and activists within these institutions, a movement can foster a cultural shift that supports its goals.

Implications

Gramsci's insights into cultural hegemony and institutional infiltration have significant implications for understanding contemporary social movements. They highlight how ideological battles are fought not only in political arenas but also within cultural spaces. This perspective has been influential in various fields, including education, sociology, and political theory, as it underscores the importance of cultural narratives in shaping social realities.

In summary, Antonio Gramsci's notion of a "Long March through the Institutions" emphasizes the importance of cultural engagement and ideological struggle within societal frameworks to achieve lasting change. This strategy seeks to transform institutions from within, ultimately aiming for a broader societal shift towards revolutionary ideals.

Conclusion

Comparing Antonio Gramsci's strategy of the "Long March through the Institutions" with the strategies of Soviet communists reveals significant differences in approach and effectiveness, particularly in the context of cultural and ideological influence.

Conversely, while the Soviet strategy achieved rapid political control in Russia, it often led to significant resistance both domestically and internationally. The reliance on force created a backlash against communist regimes, ultimately contributing to their decline in many regions by the late 20th century

The ideological goals of Gramsci and the Soviet communists were similar, but in the final analysis Gramsci's strategy can be described as the more successful. Communism exported from the Soviet Union failed and became synonymous with economic backwardness and unprecedented violence. Gramsci's strategy became successful in the West, infecting institutions and society with left-liberal ideology in all spheres.

GRAMSCI'S PREDECESSORS

Before Antonio Gramsci, several thinkers and ideologists recognized the significant power of media and culture in shaping public consciousness and political ideology.

Karl Marx

Karl Marx (1818–1883) laid the foundational ideas that influenced later thinkers like Gramsci. While primarily focused on economic structures, Marx acknowledged the role of ideology in maintaining class dominance. He introduced the concept of **"false consciousness,"** which describes how the ruling class perpetuates its ideology through cultural institutions, thus obscuring the realities of exploitation and oppression faced by the working class. Marx's analysis highlighted that media and culture could serve as tools for ideological control, even if he did not elaborate extensively on these mechanisms.

Friedrich Engels

Friedrich Engels (1820–1895), Marx's collaborator, further developed ideas regarding the interplay between culture and politics. In works like *The Origin of the Family, Private Property and the State*, Engels discussed how cultural norms and values contribute to the maintenance of class structures. He emphasized that the ruling class uses cultural institutions to propagate its values and maintain social order, thereby foreshadowing Gramsci's later concepts of hegemony.

Walter Benjamin

Walter Benjamin (1892–1940) was a German-Jewish intellectual whose work on media and culture predated Gramsci's theories. In his essay "The Work of Art in the Age of Mechanical Reproduction," Benjamin explored how mass media transforms art and culture, arguing that reproduction changes the way art is perceived and its role in society. He recognized that media could serve as a means for ideological manipulation.

John Dewey

John Dewey (1859–1952), an American philosopher and educational reformer, was aware of media's influence on public opinion. He advocated for education as a means to foster critical thinking among citizens, emphasizing that a well-informed public is essential. Dewey understood that media plays a crucial role in shaping public discourse and civic engagement. These figures contributed to an understanding of media's power long before Gramsci articulated his theories on cultural hegemony, highlighting the ongoing dialogue about ideology, culture, and power in society.

EDWARD BERNAYS AND WALTER LIPPMANN

Edward Bernays and Walter Lippmann were two pivotal figures in the early 20th century who profoundly influenced the understanding and application of media as a powerful tool for influence and propaganda. Their work laid the groundwork for modern public relations and media theory, shaping how information is disseminated and perceived in society. This chapter delves into their backgrounds, key contributions, and the implications of their ideas on media influence.

Edward Bernays: The Father of Public Relations

Edward Louis Bernays was born on November 22, 1891, in Vienna, Austria, to a Jewish family. His family immigrated to the United States when he was just a year old.

Bernays was the nephew of Sigmund Freud, which significantly influenced his later work in public relations. He graduated from Cornell University with a degree in agriculture but quickly shifted his focus to public relations and marketing after a brief stint in the grain industry.

Career and Contributions

Bernays is often referred to as the "father of public relations." He recognized early on that public opinion could be shaped through strategic communication. In 1928, he published his seminal book *Propaganda*, where he argued that public relations is essential for managing public perception in a democratic society. He famously stated:

"The conscious and intelligent manipulation of the organized habits and opinions of the masses is an important element in democratic society."

Bernays believed that those who manipulate this "unseen mechanism" of society constitute an invisible government that effectively controls public opinion. He emphasized that understanding human psychology was crucial for influencing behavior, drawing heavily on Freud's theories.

Key Campaigns

Bernays implemented several groundbreaking campaigns that exemplified his theories:

- **Torches of Freedom**: In 1929, he organized a campaign for the American Tobacco Company to encourage women to smoke by framing it as an act of liberation. During a parade in New York City, he had women march with cigarettes as "torches of freedom," linking smoking to feminist ideals. This campaign not only increased cigarette sales but also shifted societal perceptions about women's smoking.

- **Bacon and Eggs**: Bernays helped popularize bacon and eggs as the quintessential American breakfast by conducting a survey that showed people preferred this combination. He then marketed it as the "American breakfast," effectively manipulating consumer habits through strategic messaging.

- **Dixie Cups**: To promote disposable cups, Bernays linked them to sanitation concerns by creating a narrative around hygiene, which resonated with consumers during a time when cleanliness was paramount due to health crises.

Through these campaigns, Bernays demonstrated how media could be leveraged to shape public attitudes and behaviors subtly.

Legacy

Bernays' legacy is complex; while he is credited with pioneering techniques that transformed marketing and public relations, his methods also raise ethical questions about manipulation and consent. His approach laid the groundwork for modern advertising strategies, emphasizing emotional appeal over rational argumentation.

Walter Lippmann: The Public Opinion Theorist

Background

Walter Lippmann was born on September 23, 1889, in New York City. He was educated at Harvard University, where he developed an interest in journalism and political science. Lippmann became one of the most influential journalists and political commentators of his time.

Career and Contributions

Lippmann's most significant contributions came through his writings on media, democracy, and public opinion. His book *Public Opinion* (1922) critically examined how media shapes perceptions of reality. He argued that most people do not have direct experience with political events; instead, they rely on media representations to form opinions about their world.Lippmann introduced the concept of the "stereotype" in media discourse—preconceived notions that shape how individuals interpret information. He believed that these stereotypes could be manipulated by powerful interests to control public perception:

"The pictures inside our heads are not created by direct experience but are constructed from the images presented to us by the media."

Media as a Tool for Influence

Lippmann recognized that mass media could serve as both a tool for political system and a means of manipulation. He was concerned about the potential for propaganda to distort reality and mislead the public. His analysis suggested that media could create "pseudo-environments" where individuals engage with simplified narratives rather than complex realities.

Lippmann also critiqued the idea of an informed citizenry being essential for democracy, arguing that citizens often lack the knowledge or capacity to engage meaningfully with political issues due to overwhelming information. He posited that elites—journalists, politicians, and business leaders—were better equipped to interpret events and guide public opinion.

Legacy

Lippmann's work has had lasting implications for journalism and communication studies. His insights into media's role in shaping public perception continue to resonate today, particularly in discussions about misinformation and media bias in contemporary society.

The Intersection of Bernays and Lippmann

While Bernays focused on practical applications of media influence through public relations campaigns, Lippmann provided a theoretical framework for understanding how media shapes public opinion. Both recognized that media could be wielded as a powerful tool for influence:

- **Manipulation vs. Information**: Bernays viewed propaganda as a necessary tool for managing public perception positively; Lippmann warned against its potential for manipulation and misinformation.

- **Psychology and Public Opinion**: Both thinkers drew upon psychological principles—Bernays through Freud's theories on unconscious desires and Lippmann through his analysis of stereotypes—to explain how individuals respond to media messages.

- **Ethical Considerations**: Their work raises ethical questions about manipulation versus informed consent in communication practices. While Bernays believed in using these techniques for positive change, Lippmann cautioned against their potential misuse by those in power.

Conclusion

Edward Bernays and Walter Lippmann were instrumental in shaping our understanding of media as a powerful tool for influence and propaganda. Bernays' innovative approaches to public relations demonstrated how carefully crafted messages could alter consumer behavior and societal norms.

In contrast, Lippmann's critical analysis highlighted the complexities of public opinion formation in an age dominated by mass communication.Together, their contributions underscore the dual nature of media as both an instrument for enlightenment and a mechanism for control—a tension that remains relevant in today's digital landscape where information flows freely but often lacks transparency or accountability. As we navigate this complex terrain, reflecting on their legacies can help us critically assess our relationship with media and its impact on society.

JOSEPH GOEBBELS AND NAZI PROPAGANDA

Joseph Goebbels, the Minister of Propaganda for Nazi Germany, played a crucial role in shaping the narrative of the Third Reich through his mastery of media and psychological manipulation. His strategies not only facilitated the rise of Adolf Hitler but also enabled the Nazi regime to maintain control over the German populace and justify its horrific policies, including the Holocaust. This comprehensive chapter will delve into Goebbels' background, his methods of propaganda, key campaigns, psychological strategies employed, and the broader implications of Nazi propaganda.

Background of Joseph Goebbels

Early Life and Education

Joseph Goebbels was born on October 29, 1897, in Rheydt, Germany. He came from a middle-class family and was educated at the University of Heidelberg, where he earned a doctorate in philology in 1921. His early exposure to literature and philosophy shaped his understanding of language's power, which he would later exploit in his propaganda efforts. After becoming involved in politics, he joined the National Socialist German Workers' Party (NSDAP) in 1924 and quickly rose through the ranks due to his organizational skills and oratory talent.

Rise to Power

Goebbels became the Gauleiter (district leader) of Berlin in 1926, where he established a robust party organization. His ability to connect with audiences through speeches and writings earned him recognition within the Nazi Party. In 1930, he was appointed as the head of Nazi propaganda, a role that would allow him to shape public opinion on a national scale.

By 1933, when Hitler became Chancellor, Goebbels was firmly in control of the Ministry for Public Enlightenment and Propaganda.

The Role of Propaganda in Nazi Germany

Establishment of the Propaganda Ministry

Upon taking power, Goebbels transformed the Ministry for Public Enlightenment and Propaganda into a powerful tool for controlling information. The ministry oversaw all forms of media, including newspapers, radio broadcasts, films, literature, and art. Goebbels understood that controlling these channels was essential for disseminating Nazi ideology and suppressing dissenting voices.He famously stated that "the national education of the German people will be placed in my hands," reflecting his ambition to shape not only public opinion but also cultural identity. Goebbels' ministry worked tirelessly to promote Nazi ideals while censoring any material deemed contrary to their agenda.

Key Campaigns and Events

1. **The Führer Cult**: One of Goebbels' most significant achievements was creating a cult of personality around Adolf Hitler. This campaign portrayed Hitler as Germany's savior and an infallible leader. Through carefully staged rallies, such as the Nuremberg Rallies, and propaganda films like *Triumph of the Will*, Goebbels crafted an image of Hitler that emphasized strength, charisma, and national pride.

2. **Book Burnings**: In May 1933, Goebbels orchestrated public book burnings to eliminate "un-German" literature. This event symbolized the regime's commitment to controlling intellectual thought and promoting an Aryan cultural narrative. By demonizing authors who were Jewish or deemed politically undesirable, Goebbels sought to unify public sentiment against perceived enemies.

3. **Kristallnacht**: Goebbels played a pivotal role in instigating Kristallnacht (the Night of Broken Glass) on November 9-10, 1938. Following the assassination of a German diplomat by a Jewish student in Paris, Goebbels encouraged spontaneous violence against Jewish communities across Germany. This pogrom resulted in widespread destruction of synagogues and businesses and marked a significant escalation in anti-Semitic violence.

4. **War Propaganda**: As World War II progressed, Goebbels adapted his propaganda strategies to maintain morale among Germans despite military setbacks. He promoted narratives of impending victory through speeches that highlighted supposed secret weapons and historical parallels that suggested eventual triumph.

Psychological Strategies Employed by Goebbels

Goebbels' propaganda techniques were deeply rooted in psychological manipulation. He understood that effective propaganda must resonate emotionally with its audience while appealing to their fears and desires.

Manipulation of Emotions

1. **Fear Appeals**: Goebbels often utilized fear as a tool for mobilization. By portraying Jews and other minority groups as existential threats to German society, he justified extreme measures against them. This fear-based rhetoric created an environment where violence against these groups was normalized.

2. **Nationalism**: The promotion of nationalism was central to Nazi propaganda. By invoking themes of national pride and unity, Goebbels sought to galvanize support for the regime's policies. His messaging emphasized Germany's historical greatness while framing its current struggles as a result of external enemies.

3. **Scapegoating**: Jews were consistently scapegoated for Germany's economic woes and social problems. By portraying them as responsible for societal decay, Goebbels fostered public support for anti-Semitic policies and ultimately contributed to the justification for genocide.

4. **Cultivation of Loyalty**: Through repetitive messaging that glorified Hitler and demonized opponents, Goebbels cultivated loyalty among party members and ordinary citizens alike. The use of slogans like "Ein Volk, ein Reich, ein Führer" (One People, One Empire, One Leader) reinforced collective identity under Nazi ideology.

Use of Media Technologies

Goebbels was an early adopter of emerging media technologies that enhanced propaganda dissemination:

1. **Radio**: Recognizing radio's potential for reaching mass audiences, Goebbels ensured that Nazi broadcasts were pervasive throughout Germany. He understood that radio could create an intimate connection between Hitler and ordinary citizens by allowing them to hear his speeches directly.

2. **Film**: Goebbels leveraged film as a powerful medium for storytelling and persuasion. Films like *The Eternal Jew* depicted Jews as subhuman threats while glorifying Aryan ideals through state-sponsored productions like *Olympia*. These films were designed not only to entertain but also to indoctrinate viewers with Nazi ideology.

3. **Print Media**: Newspapers under Nazi control disseminated propaganda daily while censoring opposing viewpoints. The *Völkischer Beobachter*, the party's official newspaper, served as a primary source for spreading anti-Semitic rhetoric and promoting party initiatives.

The Impact of Nazi Propaganda

The effectiveness of Nazi propaganda can be seen in its profound impact on German society:

Indoctrination

Goebbels' efforts led to widespread indoctrination among Germans who accepted Nazi ideology without question. The relentless barrage of propaganda created an environment where dissent became increasingly dangerous; many citizens internalized anti-Semitic beliefs or accepted militaristic nationalism as part of their identity.

Compliance with Regime Policies

The psychological manipulation employed by Goebbels contributed significantly to compliance with Nazi policies among ordinary Germans. Many citizens participated in or turned a blind eye to atrocities committed against Jews and other marginalized groups due to their conditioning through propaganda.

Justification for War Crimes

As World War II escalated, propaganda helped justify increasingly brutal military actions against perceived enemies both abroad and at home. The portrayal of war as a noble struggle for survival resonated with many Germans who believed they were fighting for their nation's future.

Conclusion

Joseph Goebbels was instrumental in establishing Nazi propaganda as a formidable tool for influence and control over German society during one of history's darkest periods. His mastery over media technologies combined with psychological manipulation enabled the regime to spread its ideology effectively while suppressing dissenting voices.

Through campaigns that glorified Hitler and dehumanized Jews alongside other targeted groups, Goebbels fostered an environment where violence became normalized under the guise of nationalism and self-preservation. The legacy of his work serves as a chilling reminder of how powerful media can be when wielded by those who seek to manipulate public perception for nefarious ends.

Understanding this history is crucial not only for recognizing the dangers posed by propaganda but also for fostering critical engagement with media today—a lesson that remains relevant as societies continue grappling with issues related to misinformation and ideological extremism.

SOVIET PROPAGANDA

Soviet propaganda was a crucial element of the Communist regime's strategy to maintain control over the populace, promote its ideology, and justify its policies. This section will delve into the origins, evolution, and psychological strategies of Soviet propaganda, highlighting its manipulative techniques and the impact it had on Soviet society and beyond.

Origins of Soviet Propaganda

The Bolshevik Revolution

The roots of Soviet propaganda can be traced back to the Bolshevik Revolution in 1917. The new regime recognized that to consolidate power, it needed to control public perception and opinion.

Early on, Lenin emphasized the importance of propaganda as a means to communicate revolutionary ideas and mobilize the masses. He famously stated that "the press should be used as a weapon" to achieve political objectives.

The Role of the Communist Party

The Communist Party established various organizations to disseminate propaganda, including the Agitprop (Agitation and Propaganda) department. This organization was responsible for creating materials that promoted Marxist-Leninist ideology and countered anti-Bolshevik narratives. The party understood that effective propaganda was essential for fostering loyalty among the populace and suppressing dissent.

Stalin's Era

Under Joseph Stalin's leadership in the 1920s and 1930s, propaganda became even more centralized and sophisticated. Stalin utilized propaganda to cultivate a cult of personality around himself, portraying himself as the infallible leader guiding the nation toward socialism. The state-controlled media glorified his achievements while downplaying failures or dissent.

Key Features of Stalinist Propaganda

1. **Cult of Personality**: Stalin was depicted as a god-like figure whose wisdom and strength were essential for the nation's success. This portrayal was reinforced through art, literature, film, and public celebrations.

2. **Censorship**: The regime suppressed dissenting voices by censoring literature, art, and journalism that contradicted official narratives. Writers who failed to conform to party ideology faced severe consequences, including imprisonment or execution.

3. **Historical Revisionism**: Soviet propaganda often rewrote history to align with party ideology. Events such as the October Revolution were portrayed as inevitable triumphs of socialism, while opposition figures were vilified or erased from history altogether.

4. **Use of Symbols**: The hammer and sickle symbol became synonymous with communism, representing the unity of workers and peasants. Propaganda posters frequently featured bold imagery that conveyed messages of strength, unity, and progress.

Propaganda During World War II

The Second World War marked a significant turning point for Soviet propaganda. Initially caught off guard by Nazi Germany's invasion in 1941, the Soviet regime quickly mobilized its propaganda machinery to rally support for the war effort.

Key Strategies

1. **Emotional Appeals**: Propaganda during this period focused on stirring emotions such as patriotism, sacrifice, and vengeance against the enemy. The portrayal of German soldiers as brutal invaders who threatened Russian families resonated deeply with the populace.

2. **Heroic Narratives**: The Red Army's victories were celebrated through films, posters, and speeches that depicted soldiers as heroes fighting for their homeland. This narrative fostered a sense of national pride and unity against a common enemy.

3. **Use of Media**: The Soviet regime effectively utilized various media channels to disseminate propaganda. Radio broadcasts reached rural areas where literacy rates were low, while films like *The Fall of Berlin* glorified Soviet victories.

4. **Targeting Enemy Soldiers**: Psychological operations aimed at demoralizing German soldiers were also employed. Leaflets promised humane treatment upon surrender and appealed to soldiers' desires to return home to their families.

Psychological Strategies in Soviet Propaganda

Soviet propaganda employed various psychological strategies designed to manipulate perceptions and behaviors among both domestic audiences and foreign adversaries.

Emotional Manipulation

1. **Fear Appeals**: Fear was a central theme in Soviet propaganda. By portraying external enemies—capitalists, fascists—as existential threats to socialism, the regime justified its repressive measures against dissenters within society.

2. **Nationalism**: Propaganda appealed to national pride by emphasizing Russia's historical struggles against foreign invaders. This narrative fostered unity among diverse ethnic groups within the USSR while reinforcing loyalty to the state.

3. **Victimhood**: The portrayal of Soviets as victims of imperialist aggression helped galvanize support for military actions against perceived threats. This victimhood narrative resonated particularly during World War II when citizens were encouraged to view themselves as defenders of their homeland.

Stereotyping and Dehumanization

Soviet propaganda often relied on stereotypes to dehumanize perceived enemies:

1. **Class Enemies**: The regime portrayed capitalists and bourgeois elements as parasites undermining society's progress. This dehumanization justified violent purges during Stalin's era against those labeled as "class enemies."

2. **Western Imperialists**: Western nations were depicted as aggressive imperialists seeking to destroy socialism worldwide. Propaganda emphasized their supposed moral decay while promoting communism as a superior alternative.

3. **Cultural Conditioning**: Through education systems designed to instill Marxist-Leninist values from an early age, children were conditioned to view class struggle as an inherent part of life. This conditioning created a generation loyal to communist ideals without questioning state narratives.

Control Over Information

The Soviet regime exercised strict control over information dissemination:

1. **Censorship**: All media outlets were state-controlled; dissenting voices were silenced through censorship or imprisonment. This monopoly on information ensured that only approved narratives reached the public.

2. **Manipulation of Statistics**: Propaganda often manipulated statistics to present an overly positive picture of economic progress or military successes while downplaying failures or hardships faced by citizens.

3. **Creation of Myths**: Myths surrounding historical events—such as the October Revolution—were propagated through education systems and cultural narratives that emphasized heroism while omitting inconvenient truths about violence or repression.

Key Campaigns in Soviet Propaganda

Education Campaigns

Education played a vital role in shaping public perception through indoctrination:

1. **Young Pioneers**: Organizations like the Young Pioneers aimed at indoctrinating children into communist ideology from an early age through activities centered around loyalty to the party.

2. **Political Education Classes**: Schools conducted classes focused on Marxist-Leninist theory where teachers strictly adhered to state-approved curricula designed for ideological conformity rather than critical thinking skills.

3. **Cultural Events**: Festivals celebrating communist achievements served not only as entertainment but also reinforced ideological messages about collective identity and national pride.

Media Campaigns

The media served as a primary vehicle for disseminating propaganda messages:

1. **Film Production**: Films produced during Stalin's era glorified heroic figures while depicting enemies in grotesque caricatures designed for maximum emotional impact.

2. **Posters and Artwork**: Boldly designed posters with slogans like "Workers of the World Unite!" became ubiquitous throughout cities—visually reinforcing messages promoting solidarity among workers across borders.

3. **Literature Censorship**: Literature deemed contrary to socialist values faced censorship; writers who failed to conform found themselves ostracized or imprisoned—a tactic used effectively during both Stalin's purges and later periods under Brezhnev's rule.

International Propaganda Efforts

Soviet propaganda extended beyond its borders:

1. **Support for Revolutionary Movements**: The USSR actively supported revolutionary movements worldwide—offering financial aid or training—to spread communist ideology globally while portraying itself as a champion against imperialism.

2. **Cultural Diplomacy Initiatives**: Cultural exchanges showcased Soviet achievements in arts or sciences—portraying communism positively while contrasting it with capitalist decadence elsewhere.

3. **Disinformation Campaigns Against Rivals**: Disinformation tactics targeted Western nations; false narratives about social unrest within capitalist countries sought to undermine confidence in democratic systems while promoting communism's supposed superiority.

Conclusion

Soviet propaganda was an intricate system designed not just for communication but also for psychological manipulation aimed at controlling public perception both domestically and internationally throughout its existence from 1917 until 1991.

The strategies employed by propagandists included emotional appeals rooted in fear or nationalism alongside systematic dehumanization techniques targeting class enemies or Western adversaries alike.

The impact this had on shaping attitudes towards governance cannot be understated—it fostered compliance among citizens while justifying repressive measures taken by authorities against dissenters.

Soviet propaganda serves today as a cautionary tale about how powerful narratives can shape societies' beliefs—even leading them down paths toward authoritarianism if left unchecked by critical engagement with information sources available within any given context.

HERLONG, SKOUSEN AND 45 GOALS OF COMMUNISM

Albert Sydney Herlong Jr. was an American politician and lawyer known for his service as a member of the United States House of Representatives from Florida. He served ten terms from 1949 to 1969 and was a member of the Democratic Party. Herlong is particularly notable for his strong anti-communist stance and his role in promoting conservative values during a time of significant social change in the United States.

Congressional Career

In Congress, Herlong was known for his vocal opposition to communism. He introduced legislation aimed at counteracting communist propaganda and was involved in various anti-communist initiatives throughout his tenure.

One of the most notable moments in his career came on January 10, 1963, when he read into the Congressional Record a list of 45 goals of communism from W. Cleon Skousen's book *The Naked Communist*. This act was part of a broader effort to raise awareness about perceived communist threats within the United States.

The list of 45 goals

Here is an overview of the main goals interesting for our era from 45 goals as outlined by Skousen:

12. Resist any attempt to outlaw the Communist Party: This reflects a desire for legal protection for communist parties within democratic nations.

18. Gain control of all student newspapers: Controlling student media allows for shaping narratives among young people.

19. Use student riots to foment public protests against programs or organizations under Communist attack: Manipulating student activism can destabilize societal norms.

20. Infiltrate the press; gain control over book-review assignments, editorial writing, policymaking positions: Controlling media narratives is essential for shaping public opinion.

21. Gain control of key positions in radio, TV, and motion pictures: Media influence extends beyond print into audiovisual realms, impacting broader audiences.

23. Control art critics and directors of art museums. "Our plan is to promote ugliness, repulsive, meaningless art." Aesthetic control can undermine traditional cultural values.

24. Eliminate all laws governing obscenity; call them censorship violations: By promoting obscenity under free speech arguments, societal morals can be eroded.

25. Break down cultural standards of morality by promoting pornography and obscenity in media: This goal aims at normalizing behaviors that undermine traditional family structures.

26. Present homosexuality, degeneracy, and promiscuity as normal, natural, healthy.

27. Infiltrate the churches and replace revealed religion with "social" religion. Discredit the Bible and emphasize the need for intellectual maturity which does not need a "religious crutch.": Undermining religious authority can facilitate secularization aligned with communist ideals.

28. Eliminate prayer or any phase of religious expression in the schools on the ground that it violates the principle of "separation of church and state.": Removing religious expressions from public life diminishes moral frameworks based on faith.

40. Discredit the family as an institution. Encourage promiscuity and easy divorce.

41. Emphasize the need to raise children away from the negative influence of parents. Attribute prejudices, mental blocks and retarding of children to suppressive influence of parents.

Summary of the Goals

The goals outlined by Skousen include various tactics for achieving communist influence, such as:

1. **Political Manipulation**: Goals like capturing one or both major political parties in the U.S. and promoting the recognition of communist regimes highlight the strategic infiltration of political systems.

2. **Cultural Subversion**: Many goals focus on controlling education, media, and cultural institutions to promote socialist ideologies while degrading traditional American values. This includes influencing school curricula, gaining control over press narratives, and promoting obscenity and alternative lifestyles as normal.

3. **Social Engineering**: The goals emphasize changing societal norms around family structures, morality, and religion. By discrediting the family unit and promoting promiscuity and easy divorce, the intention was to weaken the traditional family as a cornerstone of society.

4. **Psychological Manipulation**: The list suggests using mental health frameworks to control dissenters and framing behavioral issues as psychiatric disorders requiring professional intervention rather than legal consequences.

5. **International Relations**: Several goals advocate for policies that would weaken American sovereignty and promote international governance through organizations like the United Nations.

Conclusion

In contemporary discussions about ideology and governance, revisiting these goals provides insight into the historical context of American political culture and the ongoing struggle between differing worldviews.

The legacy of Skousen's work continues to resonate in debates about freedom, morality, and the role of government in regulating societal norms. Understanding these dynamics is crucial for recognizing how propaganda can influence perceptions and actions within a society, highlighting the importance of critical engagement with information.

PSYCHOLOGICAL MANIPULATION IN WESTERN POLITICS OVER THE LAST CENTURY

Here are some examples of psychological manipulations in politics over the last century, reflecting various strategies used to influence public opinion, voter behavior, and political outcomes:

The Daisy Ad (1964): This infamous political advertisement for Lyndon B. Johnson's campaign used fear tactics by depicting a child counting daisies before a nuclear explosion, suggesting that Barry Goldwater's policies could lead to nuclear war.

Willie Horton Ad (1988): This ad was used by George H.W. Bush's campaign against Michael Dukakis, portraying Dukakis as soft on crime by highlighting a convicted murderer who committed crimes while on furlough, playing on racial fears and crime anxieties.

"I Like Ike" (1952): Dwight D. Eisenhower's campaign used simple, catchy slogans and relatable imagery to create a positive emotional connection with voters, effectively building a strong brand around his candidacy.

"Hope and Change" (2008): Barack Obama's campaign slogan tapped into the public's desire for optimism and a break from the past, using emotional appeals to galvanize support among young voters and disenfranchised groups.

Fear Appeals in the Cold War: Political leaders used the threat of communism and nuclear war to rally support for military spending and foreign intervention, manipulating public fears to justify aggressive policies.

Nixon's Southern Strategy: Richard Nixon's campaign capitalized on racial tensions in the South to attract white voters disillusioned by civil rights advancements, using coded language to appeal to their fears and prejudices.

"Make America Great Again" (2016): Donald Trump's slogan evoked nostalgia and a sense of loss, manipulating voters' emotions by suggesting that America had declined and needed to return to its former glory.

The "Axis of Evil" Speech (2002): George W. Bush's characterization of Iraq, Iran, and North Korea as an "axis of evil" manipulated public fear and justified military intervention in the Middle East.

Rallying Around the Flag Effect: Political leaders often use national crises (e.g., 9/11) to manipulate public sentiment and rally support for military action or increased government powers.

Voter ID Laws (2024): Efforts to ensure fair elections and prevent vote fraud have been described and labeled as "Voter Suppression" tactics and manipulating public opinion by instilling irrational fear of electoral corruption.

"Patriotism" Appeals: Politicians often manipulate national pride to garner support for military actions or controversial policies, framing dissent as unpatriotic.

"Fake News" Labeling: Politicians or media have used the term "fake news" to discredit unfavorable media coverage, manipulating public perception of the media's role and credibility.

"Tax Cuts for the Middle Class": Politicians often manipulate public sentiment by framing tax cuts as beneficial for the middle class while disproportionately favoring the wealthy.

"Crisis Management" Strategies: Political leaders often manipulate public perception during crises (e.g., natural disasters, scandals) by controlling the narrative and framing their responses as effective and decisive.

"Unity" Messaging in Polarized Times: Politicians may manipulate public sentiment by calling for unity during divisive periods, often using this rhetoric to marginalize dissent and consolidate power.

"Homosexuals suffer because of homophobia" because of Homophobia: Many politicians and activists repeat this narrative, but it is false. Orthodox Jews, for example, face attacks in the United States that are many times greater and more violent. However, they do not suffer anywhere near the rates of depression, anxiety or suicidal tendencies that homosexuals do.

"Horrible numbers" of Illegal Abortions: These manipulative statements and attacks on emotions have been and are being used by pro-abortion activists for the ability to legally murder unborn children. Several activists and abortionists (for example Bernard Nathanson) later acknowledged the manipulation of data.

These examples illustrate the various psychological manipulations employed in political contexts, highlighting how emotional appeals, fear tactics, and strategic messaging can significantly influence public opinion and political outcomes.

THE CASE OF SADDAM HUSEIN AND BIOLOGICAL WEAPONS

The case of Saddam Hussein and the alleged existence of biological weapons has been a contentious issue, particularly in the context of the U.S.-led invasion of Iraq in 2003. Despite extensive searches and inspections, no substantial evidence of active biological weapons programs was found, leading to significant debate about the intelligence that justified military action. This chapter will explore the background of Iraq's biological weapons program, the inspections conducted by international bodies, the implications of the findings, and the broader context of U.S. foreign policy.

Background of Iraq's Biological Weapons Program

Saddam Hussein's regime pursued a range of weapons of mass destruction (WMD), including biological weapons, particularly during the Iran-Iraq War in the 1980s. Reports indicated that Iraq had developed several biological agents, including anthrax and botulinum toxin, and had weaponized them for military use. The Iraqi government acknowledged some aspects of its biological weapons program in the 1990s but claimed that it had destroyed its stockpiles following the Gulf War.

UN Inspections Post-Gulf War

After Iraq's defeat in the Gulf War, United Nations Security Council Resolution 687 mandated that Iraq eliminate its WMD capabilities. The United Nations Special Commission (UNSCOM) was established to oversee inspections aimed at uncovering and dismantling Iraq's chemical and biological weapons programs. Between 1991 and 1998, UNSCOM conducted numerous inspections in Iraq. The final report from UNSCOM noted that evidence suggested an extensive biological warfare program existed prior to 1991, The report noted, that it could not be confirmed that all agents had been destroyed or that a capability did not exist afterward.

The report highlighted some discrepancies between Iraq's declarations and the physical evidence found during inspections.

The U.S.-Led Invasion and Search for WMD

In the lead-up to the 2003 invasion of Iraq, U.S. officials asserted that Saddam Hussein possessed active WMD programs that posed an immediate threat to national security. This claim was central to justifying military action against Iraq. However, as U.S. forces invaded and began searching for these weapons, no substantial stockpiles of chemical or biological agents were discovered.

Intelligence Failures

The intelligence community's assessments regarding Iraq's WMD capabilities were heavily scrutinized after the invasion. Reports indicated that while there were credible indications of past biological weapons development, there was insufficient evidence to support claims that active programs existed at the time of the invasion. Analysts pointed out that much of the intelligence used to justify military action was based on outdated or misinterpreted information.

The lack of findings led to significant criticism of the Bush administration for its reliance on flawed intelligence to justify a war that resulted in considerable human and geopolitical costs. Defense Secretary Donald Rumsfeld famously stated before the invasion that "we know where they are," referring to WMD stockpiles; however, this assertion proved unfounded as no such weapons were located.

Implications of Findings

The failure to find biological weapons in Iraq has had far-reaching implications:

1. **Credibility Crisis**: The inability to substantiate claims about Saddam Hussein's WMD capabilities damaged the credibility of U.S. intelligence agencies and eroded public trust in government assertions regarding national security threats.

2. **Impact on Foreign Policy**: It raised questions about how intelligence is gathered, analyzed, and presented.

3. **Regional Stability**: The invasion and subsequent instability in Iraq have had lasting effects on regional dynamics in the Middle East. The power vacuum created by Saddam's ousting contributed to sectarian violence and the rise of extremist groups like ISIS.

4. **Lessons Learned**: The case underscores the importance of rigorous verification processes when dealing with allegations of WMD proliferation. It highlights how political motivations can influence intelligence assessments and public discourse on national security.

Manipulation and Propaganda before the Attack

Before the 2003 invasion of Iraq, the narrative in politics and the media regarding Saddam Hussein and his alleged possession of biological weapons was characterized by a combination of fear, urgency, and a strong emphasis on national security. This narrative played a crucial role in shaping public opinion and justifying military action.

In the lead-up to the invasion, the Bush administration consistently portrayed Saddam Hussein as a significant threat to both the United States and global security. Following the September 11 attacks in 2001, there was a heightened atmosphere of fear regarding terrorism and weapons of mass destruction (WMD). The administration argued that Hussein's regime had not only developed biological weapons but also had the capability to use them against the U.S. and its allies. This framing was reinforced by claims that Iraq had links to terrorist organizations, although these connections were tenuous at best.

Key political figures, including President George W. Bush and Secretary of State Colin Powell, made public statements asserting that Iraq possessed WMDs, including biological agents like anthrax and botulinum toxin. In his now-infamous speech to the United Nations in February 2003, Powell presented what he claimed was evidence of Iraq's ongoing WMD programs, including biological weapons. This presentation aimed to rally international support for military action against Iraq.

Media Coverage

The media landscape before the invasion largely reflected and amplified the government's narrative. Major news outlets were often criticized for their lack of skepticism towards the administration's claims about Iraq's WMD capabilities. Many journalists accepted the government's assertions at face value without conducting thorough investigations or presenting opposing viewpoints.

1. **Pro-War Sentiment**: Coverage was predominantly pro-war, with many media outlets featuring military officials and government sources who supported intervention. Studies indicated that there was a significant imbalance in guest appearances on major news networks; pro-war voices outnumbered anti-war perspectives by a large margin—sometimes as much as 25 to 1.

2. **Public Perception**: As a result of this coverage, many Americans believed that Saddam Hussein was directly involved in the September 11 attacks and that he posed an imminent threat due to his alleged biological weapons stockpile. A survey conducted shortly before the invasion found that a substantial portion of the American public believed there was a direct connection between Iraq and al-Qaeda.

3. **Lack of Critical Analysis**: Critics have argued that mainstream media failed to fulfill its duty to critically analyze the government's claims about WMDs. Instead of questioning the validity of the intelligence reports or seeking independent verification, many outlets acted as conduits for government messaging. For example, The New York Times later acknowledged its shortcomings in reporting on Iraq's alleged weapons programs, admitting it should have been more aggressive in scrutinizing claims as new evidence emerged.

4. **Censorship and Control**: The U.S. military implemented embedding programs that allowed journalists to accompany troops during combat operations. While this provided firsthand accounts of military actions, it also raised concerns about censorship and control over narratives presented to the public. Journalists often faced pressure to report positively on military efforts while downplaying negative aspects such as civilian casualties or destruction.

Conclusion

The case surrounding Saddam Hussein's alleged biological weapons program remains a pivotal example of how intelligence failures can lead to significant military actions with profound consequences. While evidence suggested that Iraq had previously engaged in developing biological weapons, extensive inspections failed to confirm their existence at the time of the 2003 invasion. The ramifications extend beyond immediate military outcomes; they have reshaped public perceptions of government accountability and intelligence integrity while influencing future foreign policy decisions regarding preemptive strikes based on perceived threats.

As history continues to unfold around these events, it serves as a critical reminder of the complexities involved in international relations.

The narrative surrounding Saddam Hussein and biological weapons before the invasion of Iraq was shaped by a combination of political rhetoric and media coverage that largely aligned with government claims. This alignment fostered an environment where fear and urgency dominated public discourse, leading many Americans to support military intervention based on perceived threats from Iraq's alleged WMD capabilities.

The aftermath revealed significant gaps between these claims and reality; extensive searches conducted after the invasion found no active biological weapons programs or stockpiles. The failure to find these weapons has since prompted critical examinations of both political motivations for war and media responsibilities in reporting on national security issues. The case serves as a cautionary tale about the power of narratives in shaping public perception and policy decisions, highlighting the need for rigorous scrutiny of information presented by authorities in times of crisis.

This war based on disinformation has caused the deaths of more than a million people. Similar strategies of manipulation have been used in the conflicts in Libya, Syria and Afghanistan.

EXAMPLES OF LEVERAGED PSYCHOLOGICAL MANIPULATION IN POLITICS

Fear Appeals

Politicians often utilize fear-based messaging to highlight threats posed by opposing parties or policies. For instance, during elections, they may emphasize the potential consequences of policies on healthcare or social security, creating a sense of urgency and fear among voters about losing essential services.

Emotional Messaging

Campaigns frequently employ emotionally charged narratives to connect with voters. By sharing personal stories of individuals affected by policy changes, politicians can evoke empathy and motivate voters to support their initiatives.

Social Identity Manipulation

Some politicians has been known to frame issues in ways that resonate with specific social identities, such as race or gender. By appealing to these identities, they can galvanize support among particular demographic groups, fostering a sense of belonging and solidarity against perceived threats from opposition parties.

Disinformation and Misinformation

Similar to tactics used by other political entities, politicians have occasionally engaged in spreading misleading information about opponents or policies. This can create a distorted perception of reality that influences voter behavior, as seen with various campaign ads that exaggerate the consequences of particular policies.

Polarization Strategies

Politicians have capitalized on the increasing polarization in politics by framing their opponents as extreme or out of touch with mainstream values. This tactic not only consolidates their base but also persuades undecided voters by presenting a stark contrast between the two parties.

Nostalgia and Hope

Political messaging often invokes nostalgia for past successes under leadership of particular politicians or promises of a hopeful future. This manipulation can create a psychological anchor for voters, making them more likely to support candidates who evoke these sentiments.

Groupthink Dynamics

By promoting a narrative that emphasizes collective identity and shared values among particular politicians, party leaders can foster groupthink, where dissenting opinions are minimized. This manipulation can lead to stronger party unity and increased voter turnout.

Strategic Use of Media

Politicians strategically use media platforms to disseminate their messages while framing issues in ways that align with their political agenda. This includes using social media to target specific demographics with tailored messages that resonate on an emotional level.

Cognitive Dissonance Induction

Politicians campaigns often highlight contradictions in oponents positions or actions, creating cognitive dissonance among voters who may identify with both parties' values. This can lead individuals to realign their beliefs with particular politicians viewpoints to resolve the discomfort caused by conflicting information.

Framing and Agenda Setting

Some parties are frequently engaged in framing issues in a way that sets the agenda for public discourse. By defining problems and proposing solutions early in the conversation, they can shape public perception and influence voter priorities leading up to elections.

Conclusion

These examples illustrate how psychological manipulation techniques are employed within political strategies to influence voter behavior and perceptions effectively.

COLOUR REVOLUTIONS

The term **colour revolution** refers to a series of non-violent protests and political movements aimed at regime change, primarily in post-Soviet states. These revolutions often emerged in response to perceived electoral fraud or authoritarian governance, with the goal of establishing Western-style democracies.

The concept of colour revolutions has faced criticism, that these movements are externally orchestrated interventions aimed at destabilizing sovereign nations. Critics assert that many revolutions have been co-opted by Western interests seeking to expand their influence under the guise of promoting democracy.

Origins and Development

The origins of the colour revolution concept can be traced back to the late 1980s and early 1990s, particularly after the fall of communist regimes in Eastern Europe. Key examples include:

- The Bulldozer Revolution in Yugoslavia, which ousted Slobodan Milošević. (2000)

- Rose Revolution in Georgia. Widespread protests led to the resignation of President Eduard Shevardnadze. (2003)

- Orange Revolution in Ukraine. Protests erupted over allegations of electoral fraud in the presidential election. (2004)

- Tulip Revolution in Kyrgyzstan. Protests resulted in the ousting of President Askar Akayev. (2005)

- Velvet Revolution in Armenia (2018)

- Euromaidan (2013-2014): A series of protests in Ukraine that ultimately led to an unconstitutional coup.

- Kazakh unrest or January Events in Kazakhstan was not so successful as traditional colour revolutions in Georgia or Ukraine. The protests were fueled by a mix of economic grievances and calls for political reform rather than a unified opposition movement. The government responded with severe measures, including a state of emergency and military intervention (2022)

These events were often marked by a distinct color or symbol representing the movement, which helped unify protesters and communicate their goals.

These movements were characterized by mass mobilization, often facilitated by non-governmental organizations (NGOs) and the use of modern communication technologies, such as the internet.

The occupation of important positions in the state and in state offices or in media by their own people, or a corruption, is usually typical of both sides. The activists behind the colour revolutions portray only one side as authoritarians. The experience of several countries shows that the very part of the political forces characterised as 'democratic' has recently tryed to silencing inconvenient media (Czech Republic, Slovakia), or even to demonising and silencing alternative political parties (AfD in Germany or the EU's repression of the Orban regime in Hungary).

Mechanisms and Characteristics

Colour revolutions typically follow a pattern that includes:

1. **Public Discontent**: Triggered by unpopular governance or electoral fraud.

2. **Organized Opposition**: A united front among various opposition groups.

3. **Media Mobilization**: Effective use of the media to disseminate information about electoral irregularities or other information that may be distorted in various ways.

4. **International Support**: Often funded or supported by foreign entities hiding their interests behind propaganda about democratic reforms.

Seven Key Stages for Success

Michael McFaul identified seven key stages necessary for a successful colour revolution, which are as follows:

1. **A semi-autocratic regime**: The political environment should be characterized by a regime that is not fully autocratic, allowing for some degree of dissent and opposition.

2. **An unpopular incumbent**: The leader or ruling party must be widely regarded as unpopular, often due to perceived failures or corruption.

3. **A united and organized opposition**: There should be a cohesive and well-structured opposition group capable of mobilizing support against the incumbent.

4. **Ability to highlight electoral fraud**: The opposition must be able to quickly and effectively communicate that election results have been falsified, galvanizing public outrage.

5. **Independent media presence**: Sufficient independent media must exist to inform the populace about the alleged electoral fraud and to disseminate information supporting the opposition's narrative.

6. **Mobilization capacity**: The political opposition should be capable of organizing large-scale protests, ideally mobilizing tens of thousands of demonstrators to challenge the government's legitimacy.

7. **Divisions within coercive forces**: There must be splits or disagreements among the regime's security forces, which can undermine the government's ability to respond forcefully to protests.

These stages illustrate the complex interplay of political dynamics that can lead to significant regime change through non-violent means.

Strategies already from the 80s

Gene Sharp founded the **Albert Einstein Institution (AEI)** in the USA in 1983, through which he developed methods for organising colour revolutions around the world.

Gene Sharp's influential book is titled **From Dictatorship to Democracy**. First published in 1993, it has been widely used as a guide for organizing nonviolent resistance and has been translated into numerous languages, serving as a foundational text for various movements around the world, including Serbia's Otpor! and Georgia's Kmara.

History of the Albert Einstein Institution

- **Founding**: The AEI was established in 1983, with Sharp serving as its Senior Scholar until his death in 2018. The institution was named after Albert Einstein, who had previously endorsed Sharp's work by writing a foreword for his first book on Gandhi.

- **Mission**: The AEI's mission focuses on advancing the understanding and application of nonviolent resistance strategies. It has consulted with various pro-democracy groups worldwide, including those in Eastern Europe and the Middle East.

- **Impact**: Sharp's writings, particularly *From Dictatorship to Democracy*, have been instrumental in numerous nonviolent movements globally. The institution has provided training and resources to activists in over 65 countries, emphasizing the effectiveness of nonviolent methods in political struggles.

- **Funding Challenges**: In 2004, the AEI faced significant funding cuts, which reduced its annual income drastically. Consequently, it began operating from Sharp's home in East Boston with a minimal staff.

- **Legacy**: Despite financial constraints, the AEI has continued to disseminate its materials freely online, allowing activists around the world to access critical strategies for nonviolent resistance. Sharp's influence persists through the ongoing use of his texts in various movements referring to democracy and human rights.

Main Thoughts from Gene Sharp Book

Gene Sharp's book From Dictatorship to Democracy outlines a strategic framework for nonviolent resistance against oppressive regimes. Here are the key thoughts and concepts presented in the book:

Core Concepts

Nonviolent Action as a Technique: Sharp emphasizes that nonviolent action is a strategic method of struggle that utilizes psychological, social, economic, and political power to challenge and dismantle authoritarian systems. He argues that individuals can effectively resist oppression without resorting to violence, which often leads to further conflict and suffering.

Withdrawal of Consent: A central theme is the idea that all political power relies on the consent and cooperation of the governed. Sharp posits that if enough people withdraw their support—be it through noncooperation or protest—the regime's authority will weaken, potentially leading to its collapse.

Types of Nonviolent Action: The book categorizes nonviolent actions into three main types:

- *Protest and Persuasion:* This includes public demonstrations, speeches, and symbolic acts aimed at raising awareness and mobilizing support.

- *Noncooperation:* This can be social (e.g., boycotts), economic (e.g., strikes), or political (e.g., civil disobedience). The goal is to disrupt the normal functioning of the oppressive system.

- *Intervention:* This involves direct actions such as sit-ins or establishing alternative institutions to challenge the status quo.

Strategies for Success

Creativity in Tactics: Sharp encourages activists to be innovative in their approaches. He provides a comprehensive list of 198 methods for nonviolent action, urging groups to select tactics that suit their specific context and goals. This arsenal includes everything from symbolic gestures to organized strikes.

Understanding Opponent Dynamics: The effectiveness of nonviolent action often hinges on creating a dilemma for the oppressor: if they respond violently, they risk losing public sympathy; if they do not respond, they appear weak.

Realism about Challenges: Sharp acknowledges the difficulties faced by those who choose nonviolent resistance, including potential repression and violence from authorities. He stresses that while nonviolent strategies do not guarantee success, they offer a viable alternative to armed struggle.

Overall, *From Dictatorship to Democracy* serves as both a theoretical framework and a practical guide for activists seeking to effect change through nonviolent means. Sharp's insights have influenced numerous movements worldwide, demonstrating the potential power of organized, strategic nonviolence in their political struggle.

SERBIA'S OTPOR!

Otpor! (meaning "Resistance" in Serbian) was a pivotal nonviolent movement founded in 1998 by a group of university students in Serbia, primarily at the University of Belgrade. The organization emerged in response to the regime of Slobodan Milošević, who had been in power since 1989.

Origins and Goals

Initially, Otpor! was formed to protest against new laws that curtailed university autonomy and more control of the press. The group quickly evolved into a broader movement aimed at mobilizing citizens against the Milošević regime, advocating for democracy and human rights. Otpor! sought to shift the political culture in Serbia by encouraging civic engagement.

Strategies and Tactics

Otpor! distinguished itself through creative and humorous tactics, which included:

- **Satirical Protests**: They organized street theater and visual protests that mocked the regime. For example, during a fundraising initiative by the government, Otpor! set up a barrel for people to donate money to "Milosević's retirement," allowing citizens to symbolically hit the barrel as a form of protest.

- **Nonviolent Training**: The organization provided training workshops on civil disobedience and nonviolent resistance, empowering citizens to participate actively in the movement.

- **Grassroots Mobilization**: Otpor! expanded its reach beyond student activism, involving everyday citizens across Serbia. At its peak, it boasted around 70,000 active supporters.

Impact on Politics

The culmination of Otpor!'s efforts came during the 2000 elections when they played a crucial role in mobilizing mass protests against electoral fraud. Their slogan "Gotov je!" ("He is finished!") became emblematic of the campaign to oust Milošević. In October 2000, widespread demonstrations led to his resignation, marking a significant victory for Otpor! and the Democratic Opposition of Serbia (DOS).

Later Democratic Opposition of Serbia (DOS) lost power due to a combination of internal divisions, public disillusionment, failure to deliver promises, corruption and governance issues.

Although Milošević was accused of many crimes, he was never legally convicted, he died of a heart attack. The trial against him began on 12 February 2002 and lasted until his death on 11 March 2006.

Following Milošević's fall, Otpor! transitioned into a watchdog organization focused on government accountability before eventually dissolving in 2004. Members like Srđa Popović became influential figures in promoting nonviolent movements worldwide. The strategies developed by Otpor! have inspired similar movements across various countries.

Two leading youth movements, namely Kmara in Georgia and Pora in Ukraine, were strongly inspired by the Serbian Otpor movement. Otpor veterans personally trained Georgian and Ukrainian activists in protest procedures and actively helped to structure and define the campaign strategies of their movements. For example, the idea of bringing Serbian and Georgian activists together was born in the Tbilisi offices of the National Democratic Institute and the Open Society Foundation.

Activists in post-Soviet states, especially in Ukraine, not only took their cue from Otpor, but also drew on the experience of Slovak activists who helped the opposition defeat Prime Minister Vladimir Mečiar in the 1998 elections.

Georgian and Ukrainian activists have seen that similar ways of doing things produce similar results, despite the structural differences between the countries.

A key factor in the success of mobilisation in Georgia and Ukraine was financial assistance from the West to local civil society organisations involved in organising protests. The national campaigns of individual movements would not have been possible without external funding.

This is targeted interference by Western countries in the internal affairs of other states.

ARAB SPRING

Colour revolutions, characterized by mass protests and non-violent resistance aimed at regime change, have had significant occurrences in Muslim-majority countries, particularly during the Arab Spring. This series of uprisings began in late 2010 and spread across the Arab world, drawing parallels to earlier colour revolutions in Eastern Europe.

The Arab Spring as a Colour Revolution

The Arab Spring is often considered a manifestation of the colour revolution phenomenon within Muslim countries. It began with the Tunisian Revolution on December 18, 2010, leading to the ousting of President Zine El Abidine Ben Ali. This event was to inspire widespread protests across the region, including:

- **Egypt**: The protests culminated in the resignation of President Hosni Mubarak on February 11, 2011.

- **Libya**: The uprising against Muammar Gaddafi led to a civil war and his death in October 2011.

- **Syria**: Initial protests escalated into a brutal civil war beginning in March 2011.

- **Yemen**: Protests resulted in the resignation of President Ali Abdullah Saleh in February 2012.

- **Turkey**: While the Gezi Park protests in 2013 were significant in highlighting public discontent with Erdoğan's regime, they did not lead to a successful color revolution or regime change in Turkey.

Outcomes

While these uprisings initially succeeded in toppling long-standing leaders, the aftermath has been complex and often disillusioning:

- **Political Instability**: Many countries faced significant instability post-uprisings. Tunisia, for instance, has experienced frequent changes in government and ongoing economic challenges despite being viewed as a relative success story.

- **Civil Conflict**: In Libya and Syria, revolutions devolved into protracted civil wars, leading to humanitarian crises and regional instability. The Islamic State (ISIS) expanded into Syria, after it emerged from a complex interplay of different factors, primarily rooted in the aftermath of the U.S. invasion of Iraq in 2003.

- **Authoritarian Resurgence**: Some nations saw a return to authoritarian practices or the emergence of new authoritarian regimes.

International Perspectives

The role of external actors has been contentious. Critics argue that Western nations have sometimes exploited these movements for geopolitical interests, leading to accusations of orchestrating instability under the guise of promoting democracy.

This perspective is echoed by many nations that view colour revolutions as tools of Western hegemony aimed at destabilizing regions for strategic gain.

CAMBRIDGE ANALYTICA

Cambridge Analytica was a political consulting firm that became infamous for its role in data misuse during major political campaigns, particularly the 2016 U.S. presidential election and the Brexit referendum. Founded in 2013 as a subsidiary of the SCL Group, it specialized in data analytics and psychological profiling to influence voter behavior.

Origins and Methodology

Cambridge Analytica was established to leverage data science techniques for political consulting. Its methods were rooted in a 2010 Facebook feature rollout called Open Graph, which allowed developers to access user data more extensively than before.

This capability was exploited by Aleksandr Kogan, a researcher at the University of Cambridge, who created an app called "This Is Your Digital Life." The app collected personal data from users who took a personality quiz and also harvested data from their Facebook friends, resulting in information from approximately 87 million profiles being accessed without explicit consent.

The firm utilized this extensive dataset to create detailed psychological profiles of potential voters, allowing for highly targeted advertising campaigns. This practice, known as microtargeting, aimed to tailor political messages based on individual personality traits and preferences.

Rise to Prominence

Cambridge Analytica gained significant attention for its involvement in high-profile political campaigns. It played a crucial role in Donald Trump's presidential campaign and the Leave campaign during the Brexit referendum. The firm claimed to have developed strategies that effectively influenced voter decisions through tailored messaging based on psychological insights.

The company's notoriety peaked in March 2018 when investigative reports revealed its data practices. Whistleblower Christopher Wylie disclosed that Cambridge Analytica had misused Facebook data to manipulate electoral outcomes, leading to widespread public outrage and calls for accountability from both Facebook and Cambridge Analytica.

Legal and Political Fallout

Following these revelations, Cambridge Analytica faced intense scrutiny. Facebook suspended the firm's access to its platform and initiated investigations into its data practices. Mark Zuckerberg testified before Congress regarding Facebook's role in the scandal, which resulted in significant fines for the company due to privacy violations.

Cambridge Analytica ultimately filed for bankruptcy in May 2018 amidst growing legal challenges and reputational damage.

Despite its closure, the scandal sparked ongoing debates about data privacy, ethical marketing practices, and the influence of social media on democracy. The fallout continues to shape discussions around regulation and oversight of digital platforms today.

Campaign Coordination and Ad Creation

Documents revealed that Cambridge Analytica produced in Donald Trump's 2016 presidential campaign over 5,000 ad campaigns, generating approximately 1.5 billion impressions across various digital platforms. The firm claimed that its ads contributed to a 3% increase in favorability for Trump and drove a 2% increase in absentee ballot submissions.

Notably, Cambridge Analytica also coordinated efforts with the pro-Trump Super PAC "Make America Number 1," which raised concerns about illegal coordination between the PAC and the Trump campaign.

Steve Bannon, a key figure in the Trump campaign who had previously worked with Cambridge Analytica, was instrumental in integrating the firm's data-driven strategies into the campaign's overall approach. Bannon's connections facilitated access to the firm's services, which were critical for crafting effective messaging and voter outreach efforts.

RUSSIAN HACKERS

During the 2016 U.S. presidential elections, the narrative about Russian interference was characterized by these key information and misinformation:

Russian military intelligence (GRU) conducted extensive hacking operations targeting the Democratic National Committee (DNC), the Clinton campaign, and other Democratic organizations. They gained access to sensitive emails and documents, which were later released through platforms like WikiLeaks to damage Clinton's candidacy.

The Internet Research Agency (IRA) played a crucial role in spreading disinformation on social media. They created fake accounts to disseminate divisive content, promote hashtags like #Hillary4Prison, and stage rallies that appeared to be grassroots movements supporting Trump while disparaging Clinton.

The Russian efforts was to include a sophisticated social media strategy aimed at sowing discord among American voters. It was to involve the posting inflammatory content on platforms such as Facebook, Twitter, and Instagram, targeting various social issues to polarize public opinion.

Reports from U.S. intelligence agencies contained that the interference was ordered by Russian President Vladimir Putin, with the goal of disrupting American democracy and supporting Trump's election.

Mueller Investigation Outcomes

The investigation into Russian interference in the 2016 U.S. presidential election was led by **Robert Mueller**, a former FBI director. He was appointed as special counsel by **Deputy Attorney General Rod Rosenstein** in May 2017, following the recusal of Attorney General Jeff Sessions from matters related to the investigation due to his contacts with Russian officials.

Mueller's mandate included overseeing the FBI's existing investigation into Russian interference and examining any links or coordination between the Trump campaign and the Russian government. His investigation concluded in March 2019, resulting in a comprehensive report detailing various findings.

Ultimately, insufficient evidence was found to prove conspiracy or coordination with the Russian government. Claims of Russian hacking activities turned out to be a bunch of purposeful manipulations.

PSY-GROUP

Psy-Group was a private intelligence agency based in Israel, known for its controversial operations in online perception management and social media manipulation. Founded by Joel Zamel, the company gained notoriety for its involvement in various high-profile political campaigns and investigations, including connections to Cambridge Analytica.

Key Features of Psy-Group

- **Operations**: Psy-Group specialized in a range of activities including:

  - **Online perception management**: Crafting narratives and influencing public opinion through social media.

  - **Opposition research**: Gathering damaging information on political opponents.

  - **Clandestine activities**: Engaging in covert operations which included honey traps and other forms of espionage.

- **Notable Projects**:

  - **Project Butterfly**: Launched in 2016, this initiative targeted Boycott, Divestment, and Sanctions (BDS) activists on U.S. college campuses by collecting derogatory information about them.

- **Collaboration with Cambridge Analytica**: Psy-Group signed a memorandum with Cambridge Analytica in December 2016, which was later scrutinized during investigations into foreign interference in U.S. elections.

- **Leadership**: The CEO, Royi Burstein, was a former lieutenant colonel in the Israel Defense Forces, which highlighted the military background prevalent among its staff.

The company's strategies also included using digital platforms to reach voters with digital campaigns, including social media and online advertising. They were able to reach different demographic groups and tailor content to their preferences.

Campaigns focused on creating an emotional connection with voters. This was done through stories and personal experiences that resonated with citizens, reinforcing feelings of trust and identification with the chosen candidates.

Data analysis was applied to track voter reactions. Based on this, campaign content was adapted in real time. In this way, it was possible to respond to current trends and changing voters' views, increasing the relevance of their outreach.

The company worked with influencers and public figures, extending the reach of the campaign and reaching a wider audience.

Psy-Group articulated a clear vision and values for the candidates that voters see as important and perceive as positive factors in building a strong image of a candidate who is capable of leading the country forward into the future.

Closure and Legacy

Psy-Group ceased operations amid investigations led by Special Counsel Robert Mueller concerning election interference. The agency's activities raised significant ethical questions about the use of private intelligence firms in political processes and the implications for democracy and privacy.

Psy-Group's legacy is marked by its innovative yet controversial approaches to intelligence and influence, reflecting broader trends in modern information warfare and information operations.

GOOGLE

Google's approach to censorship has been a contentious issue, drawing criticism from various quarters for its perceived biases and compliance with governmental demands. This overview will explore the history, mechanisms, and implications of Google's censorship practices.

Historical Context

Early Censorship Practices

Google's censorship practices began almost simultaneously with its inception, primarily focusing on spam and copyright violations. The company has historically removed sites that violate its guidelines, even without direct government orders.

A notable example is compliance with the U.S. Digital Millennium Copyright Act (DMCA), which mandates the removal of copyrighted content globally, despite being a U.S. law.

International Compliance

Google has also adapted its services to comply with local laws in various countries. For instance, in Germany, Google is prohibited from displaying Nazi-related content. This localized censorship has raised concerns about the consistency and fairness of Google's policies across different regions.

Recent Developments

Global Censorship Orders

In recent years, courts have begun to assert that Google can be compelled to remove search results on a global scale. A 2017 Canadian Supreme Court ruling stated that Google must comply with such orders worldwide, prompting fears about the implications for freedom of expression and potential overreach by governments.

Political Allegations

Accusations of political bias have intensified, particularly among conservative groups who claim that Google suppresses their viewpoints. This sentiment was echoed by President Donald Trump and others who argue that Google's algorithms favor liberal content over conservative perspectives.

Investigations have shown that liberal websites tend to receive more organic traffic than their conservative counterparts, further fueling these claims.

Mechanisms of Censorship

Algorithmic Bias and Content Moderation

Google's search algorithms are often criticized for promoting certain narratives while sidelining others. Critics argue that this creates an "ideological echo chamber," where only mainstream or politically correct views are amplified.

Additionally, Google has faced scrutiny for its content moderation practices on platforms like YouTube, where it has been accused of disproportionately targeting conservative voices.

Implications for Free Speech

The ongoing debate surrounding Google's censorship practices raises critical questions about free speech in the digital age. While the company asserts that it aims to provide relevant and safe content, critics argue that its actions can lead to significant restrictions on diverse viewpoints. The challenge lies in balancing compliance with local laws while safeguarding users' rights to access a broad spectrum of information.

Google has been criticised for manipulating search results, which includes displaying negative narratives about selected politicians and suppressing positive coverage of these individuals. Autocomplete, whose designs are perceived as interfering with elections and showing bias against conservative figures, has also been criticised.

In the context of these facts, statements are being made that it is not Russia but Google and Facebook that pose the greatest threat to free and fair democratic elections.

FACEBOOK

Note: In early 2025, Mark Zuckerberg announced that Facebook was ending with progressive fact-checkers. It's questionable how this will ultimately play out. The following information about manipulation and censorship relates to the period before 2025.

Censorship on Facebook has become a contentious issue, reflecting broader debates about free speech, misinformation, and the platform's role as a modern public square. The complexities of Facebook's content moderation policies have led to significant criticism and scrutiny from various stakeholders, including civil rights organizations, governments, and users.

Overview of Facebook's Censorship Policies

Facebook employs a range of content moderation strategies aimed at regulating what is deemed acceptable speech on its platform.

These policies are often criticized for being inconsistent and opaque. For instance, while the platform aims to remove content that incites violence or hate speech, it has faced backlash for censoring legitimate political discourse and marginalized voices.

Critics argue that the platform's algorithms and human moderators frequently misinterpret context, leading to unjustified removals of content that does not violate any laws or community standards.

Key Issues in Censorship

- **Inconsistent Enforcement**: Reports indicate that Facebook has inconsistently enforced its policies, particularly regarding political content. For example, posts critical of certain governments or political movements have been disproportionately removed or restricted. This has raised concerns about bias in moderation practices.

- **Impact on Marginalized Voices**: Activists from marginalized communities have reported that their posts are more likely to be censored compared to similar content from users in more privileged positions. This has led to accusations that Facebook's moderation practices perpetuate systemic inequalities.

- **Government Pressure**: In various countries, Facebook has faced pressure from governments to censor specific types of speech. For instance, in Germany, the platform actively censors anti-immigrant. Similarly, during conflicts involving Israel and Palestine, accusations have emerged that Facebook disproportionately censors pro-Palestinian content.

- **User Experiences**: Many users have shared experiences of having their content removed without clear explanations. This lack of transparency contributes to a sense of mistrust towards the platform's moderation decisions. High-profile cases include politicians like Elizabeth Warren facing censorship for critical posts about Facebook itself and individuals like Qasim Rashid reporting removals related to discussions on human rights issues.

Legal and Ethical Considerations

The intersection of censorship and free speech raises important legal questions. While Facebook is a private entity not bound by the First Amendment, its role as a major communication platform places it at the center of debates about public discourse and censorship rights. Organizations like the ACLU argue that private companies should exercise restraint in moderating speech to avoid infringing on democratic principles.

Calls for Reform

Advocates for reform are pushing for greater transparency in how Facebook moderates content. They argue for clearer guidelines on what constitutes acceptable speech and a more robust process for users to contest censorship decisions. Recent legal challenges in various jurisdictions highlight the need for platforms like Facebook to establish fairer practices regarding content moderation.

Conclusion

Censorship on Facebook is a multifaceted issue that intertwines with broader societal debates about free speech, equality, and the responsibilities of tech giants in moderating online discourse. As the platform continues to evolve its policies, ongoing dialogue among users, advocacy groups, and policymakers will be crucial in shaping a more equitable digital landscape.

BIG TECH, NGO'S AND ABORTIONS IN IRELAND

This example is in fact representative of many other manipulative and often anti-democratic practices in various campaigns today. Similar strategies where Big Tech companies and NGOs come together to influence public opinion are not uncommon.

Ireland was pressured by outside forces to abolish the Eighth Amendment, which protected life at all stages, including the unborn. There existed the interference from Big Tech and globalist groups. Meanwhile, the mainstream media and social media companies like Google and Facebook were directly involved in swaying people's opinions to favor voting to repeal the pro-life constitution.

It was a serious interference in democracy, which has never been addressed by the authorities in this country. George Soros, Bank of America, Ford Foundation and other globalists played a significant role in changing the Irish culture away from its traditions by directly funding pro-abortion projects and groups. Thay attempted to discredit pro-lifers and the Eighth Amendment.

Big Tech's Influence

During the abortion referendum in Ireland in 2018, pro-life campaigners expressed strong criticism against Google for its decision to ban campaign advertisements. This ban was perceived as an attempt to silence pro-life voices and skew the referendum's outcome. Also Facebook later restricted such activities.

Censorship Allegations

Pro-life advocates argued that Google's ban amounted to censorship, limiting their ability to communicate their message effectively during a critical time. They felt this decision disproportionately affected their campaign compared to pro-abortion groups, which continued to run ads.

Critics contended that restricting political advertising undermined democratic processes. They claimed that such actions by tech giants like Google could influence the referendum's results by creating an uneven playing field.

Foreign Influence

Some pro-life groups highlighted concerns that the ban favored foreign pro-abortion organizations that were actively campaigning in Ireland, thereby raising questions about the integrity of local democratic engagement.

The ban sparked significant public backlash, with many viewing it as an example of Silicon Valley's growing control over political discourse. Pro-life supporters labeled the decision "outrageous" and called for greater accountability from tech companies regarding their role in political campaigns.

Conclusion

This controversy underscored broader discussions about the influence of social media platforms on political issues and the responsibilities of these companies in managing political content.

Ireland's economic reliance on Big Tech complicates regulatory efforts and requiring compliance with the rules.

ARTIFICAL INTELLIGENCE

Critiques of artificial intelligence (AI), particularly regarding perceived biases favoring left-liberal narratives, have become increasingly prominent. Various studies and expert opinions highlight concerns that AI models like ChatGPT exhibit systematic political biases, often aligning with left-leaning ideologies.

Findings from Research

Systematic Left-Wing Bias: A significant study conducted by researchers at the University of East Anglia (UEA) claimed that ChatGPT demonstrates a "systematic" left-wing bias. This research indicated that responses from the AI favored political beliefs associated with the Labour Party in the UK and the Democratic Party in the US.

The study involved asking ChatGPT politically charged questions and comparing its default responses to those when prompted to adopt specific political identities, revealing a consistent alignment with left-leaning perspectives.

Political Orientation Tests: In tests involving 14 different AI chatbots, ChatGPT was identified as the most left-leaning. The findings suggested that responses to politically sensitive statements were predominantly classified as left-leaning across various models, raising alarms about the potential influence of such biases on public discourse and policymaking.

Concerns Over Misinformation: Critics argue that the embedded liberal biases in AI could lead to misinformation and a skewed representation of facts. Experts from conservative think tanks have expressed worries that these biases might degrade democratic processes by shaping public perceptions in ways that favor one political ideology over another.

Implications for Media and Society

Impact on Journalism: There are fears that AI tools like ChatGPT could exacerbate existing biases in journalism, where media outlets have been accused of drifting towards liberal narratives. This shift could undermine the trustworthiness of news, as AI-generated content may not adequately represent diverse viewpoints.

Censorship and Cultural Wars: Right-wing commentators have accused AI models of censoring conservative viewpoints, arguing that the training data predominantly reflects liberal sources. This situation has led to assertions that AI technologies perpetuate a "woke" agenda, further polarizing societal debates.

Need for Transparency: The lack of transparency regarding AI training sets has been criticized, as companies often do not disclose the data sources used to train their models. This opacity raises questions about accountability and the potential for biases to go unchecked within these powerful technologies.

Conclusion

The discourse surrounding AI and its political biases underscores a broader cultural conflict between left-liberal and conservative ideologies. As reliance on AI tools grows, it becomes crucial to scrutinize their outputs and ensure that they do not perpetuate existing biases or distort public understanding of political issues. The ongoing debate highlights the need for more rigorous testing and transparency in AI development to foster a balanced representation of diverse perspectives in society.

ENDNOTES

In today's media and internet landscape, it is crucial to approach information with a critical mindset, particularly regarding media manipulation and political propaganda. The pervasive nature of these tactics can significantly distort public perception and influence societal attitudes.

Media manipulation involves orchestrated efforts to mislead or misinform the public, often through the use of disinformation and propaganda techniques. These tactics exploit the features of mass communication and digital platforms to create narratives that serve specific interests.

For instance, actors may employ rhetorical strategies, logical fallacies, and selective presentation of facts to shape opinions while suppressing dissenting viewpoints.

This manipulation can manifest in various forms, such as astroturfing—where fake grassroots movements are created to simulate public support for a cause—and propaganda laundering, which involves using less credible sources to propagate dubious claims without accountability.

Political spin, another facet of media manipulation, seeks to control narratives by presenting information in a biased manner that favors a particular agenda. This practice often involves carefully crafted messaging designed to evoke specific emotional responses from the audience, thereby skewing their understanding of issues.

The rise of social media has exacerbated these issues, as algorithms and automation allow for rapid dissemination of manipulated content on a global scale, making it increasingly difficult for individuals to discern fact from fiction.

To navigate this complex landscape, individuals must cultivate media literacy skills that enable them to critically analyze sources and question the motives behind the information presented. Educational institutions play a vital role in this regard by equipping students with the tools necessary to identify misinformation and understand the dynamics of propaganda.

By fostering a culture of skepticism and inquiry, society can mitigate the effects of media. In conclusion, while media serves as a powerful tool for communication and information dissemination, it is essential to recognize that not all content is created equal. By remaining vigilant and discerning in our consumption of media, we can protect ourselves from manipulation and contribute to a more informed public discourse.

REFERENCES

Gramsci, Antonio. *Selections from the Prison Notebooks of Antonio Gramsci*. Edited by Quintin Hoare and Geoffrey Nowell-Smith. New York: International Publishers, 1971.

Hoare, George, and Nathan Sperber. *An Introduction to Antonio Gramsci: His Life, Thought and Legacy*. London: Bloomsbury Academic, 2015. ISBN: 9781472572769.

Sperber, Jonathan. *Karl Marx: A Nineteenth-Century Life*. New York: Liveright Publishing, 2013. ISBN: 9780871407375.

Green, John. *Friedrich Engels: A Biography*. London: Macmillan, 1978. ISBN: 9780333191948.

Bernays, Edward L. *Biography of an Idea: Memoirs of Public Relations*. New York: Simon & Schuster, 1965. ISBN: 9780671622018.

Tye, Larry. *The Father of Spin: Edward L. Bernays and the Birth of Public Relations*. New York: Picador, 1998. ISBN: 9780805067897.

Steel, Ronald. *Walter Lippmann: A Biography*. New York: Harcourt Brace Jovanovich, 1980. ISBN: 9780151747509.

Bennett, David H. *The Lippmann Report: The Great Journalist's Legacy*. New York: Columbia University Press, 2019. ISBN: 9780231182570.

Longerich, Peter. *Goebbels: A Biography*. New York: Random House, 2015. ISBN: 9781400067513.

Goebbels, Joseph. *The Goebbels Diaries, 1939-1941*. Edited by Louis P. Lochner. New York: Doubleday, 1948. ISBN: 9780385073882.

Welch, David. *Nazi Propaganda: The Power and the Limitations*. London: Bloomsbury Academic, 2017. ISBN: 9781474290409.

Shultz, Richard H., and Roy Godson. *Dezinformatsia: Active Measures in Soviet Strategy*. Washington, D.C.: Pergamon-Brassey's, 1984. ISBN: 9780080301815.

Kenez, Peter. *The Birth of the Propaganda State: Soviet Methods of Mass Mobilization, 1917-1929*. Cambridge: Cambridge University Press, 1985. ISBN: 9780521311774.

Berkhoff, Karel C. *Motherland in Danger: Soviet Propaganda during World War II*. Cambridge, MA: Harvard University Press, 2012. ISBN: 9780674049246.

Skousen, W. Cleon. The Naked Communist: Exposing Communism and Restoring Freedom. Salt Lake City: Izzard Ink Publishing, 2017. ISBN: 9781630729233.

Marx, Karl, and Friedrich Engels. *The Communist Manifesto*. London: Penguin Classics, 2002. ISBN: 9780140447576.

Lyons, Eugene. *The Red Decade: The Challenge of Communism in America*. New York: Harcourt, Brace and Company, 1941. ISBN: 9780151760669.

Riker, William H. *The Art of Political Manipulation*. New Haven: Yale University Press, 1986. ISBN: 9780300035929.

Le Cheminant, Wayne, and John M. Parrish, eds. *Manipulating Democracy: Democratic Theory, Political Psychology, and Mass Media*. New York: Routledge, 2018. ISBN: 9780415878050.

Hamza, Khidir. *Saddam's Secrets: How an Iraqi General Defied and Survived Saddam Hussein*. New York: Scribner, 2001. ISBN: 9780743200210.

Zilinskas, Raymond A. *Iraq's Biological Weapons: The Past as Future?* JAMA, vol. 278, no. 5, 1997, pp. 418–424. doi:10.1001/jama.1997.03550050080037.

Mitchell, Lincoln A. *The Color Revolutions*. Philadelphia: University of Pennsylvania Press, 2012. ISBN: 9780812207095.

Esposito, John L., and James P. Piscatori, eds. *Color Revolutions and the Arab Spring: A Comparative Perspective*. New York: Oxford University Press, 2014. ISBN: 9780199325034.

Runciman, David. *The New Authoritarianism: Trump, Putin, Erdogan, and the Threat to Democracy*. London: Profile Books, 2022. ISBN: 9781788167173.

Wylie, Christopher. *Mindf*ck: Cambridge Analytica and the Plot to Break America**. New York: Knopf, 2019. ISBN: 9781984854636.

Kaiser, Brittany. *Targeted: My Inside Story of Cambridge Analytica and How Trump and Facebook Broke Democracy*. New York: HarperCollins, 2019. ISBN: 9780062876486.

Mueller, Robert S. *The Mueller Report: The Final Report of the Special Counsel into Donald Trump, Russia, and Collusion*. Washington, D.C.: U.S. Department of Justice, 2019. ISBN: 9780160918509.

Isikoff, Michael, and David Corn. *Russian Roulette: The Inside Story of Putin's War on America and the Election of Donald Trump*. New York: Twelve, 2018. ISBN: 9781538728741.

Cadwalladr, Carole. *The Manipulators: The Story of the Cambridge Analytica Scandal.* London: Fourth Estate, 2020. ISBN: 9780008390132.

Schneier, Bruce. *Data and Goliath: The Hidden Battles to Collect Your Data and Control Your World.* New York: W. W. Norton & Company, 2015. ISBN: 9780393352177.

Vorhies, Zach, and Kent Heckenlively. *Google Leaks: A Whistleblower's Exposé of Big Tech Censorship.* New York: Skyhorse Publishing, 2021. ISBN: 9781510767362.

Kaye, David. *The New Censorship: Inside the Global Battle for Media Freedom.* New York: Columbia Global Reports, 2021. ISBN: 9780999745489.

Kaye, David. *Speech Police: The Global Struggle to Govern the Internet.* New York: Columbia Global Reports, 2019. ISBN: 9780999745489.

Hartwig, Ryan, and Kent Heckenlively. *Behind the Mask of Facebook: A Whistleblower's Shocking Story of Big Tech Bias and Censorship.* New York: Skyhorse Publishing, 2021. ISBN: 9781510767942.

Tim Jackson. Documentary film: *IRELAND'S FALL: THE ABORTION DECEPTION - How the Elites Killed the Right to Life.* Publisher, 2018.

Harris, Tom. "OpenAI's ChatGPT Accused of Left-Wing Bias Favoring Labour and Democrats." The Telegraph, August 17, 2023. telegraph.co.uk/business/2023/08/17/openai-chatgpt-left-wing-bias-labour-party-democrats/.

Wulfsohn, Joseph A. "ChatGPT Critics Fear Artificial Intelligence Tool Liberal Biases Pushes Left-Wing Talking Points." Fox Business, October 10, 2024. foxbusiness.com/media/chatgpt-critics-fear-artificial-intelligence-tool-liberal-biases-pushes-left-wing-talking-points.

Šimečka, Michal. *Difúzia a mobilizácia občianskej spoločnosti vo farebných revolúciách*, Nuffield College, University of Oxford, 2009.

Psychology and Manipulation in Politics and Media